CRYSTAL
COLORING BOOK

This Coloring Book not only help you to relieve stress and pressure in life.
They are also a companion with you when you need to share.
Color your life more fresh. Have fun coloring together!

COLORING BOOK

THIS BOOK BELONGS TO

_____

_____

_____

COLOR TEST PAGE

Coloring

Diamond

Love Diamonds

ICOLORMYLIFE

THANK FOR TRUSTING
AND CHOOSING OUR PRODUCT

VISIT OUR WEBSITE TO GET MORE FREE WONDERFUL PRODUCTS

SCAN ME

HTTPS://ICOLORMYLIFE.COM/FREE-PRINT

ICOLORMYLIFE.COM

Printed in Great Britain
by Amazon